SPEED MACHINES

PORSCHE

Simon Mulligan

PowerKiDS press.
New York

Published in 2013 by The Rosen Publishing Group, Inc.
29 East 21st Street, New York, NY 10010

First Edition

Editor: Jennifer Way
Book Design: Greg Tucker

Photo Credits: Cover, pp. 4, 8, 13, 17, 20, 24, 25 Max Earey/Shutterstock.com; p. 5 (top) Marilyn Barbone/Shutterstock.com; pp. 5 (bottom), 10 Natali Glado/Shutterstock.com; p. 6 © SuperStock/age fotostock; p. 7 Keystone/Hulton Archive/Getty Images; p. 9 Car Culture/Getty Images; pp. 11, 23 © Hans Dieter Seufert/c/age fotostock; p. 12 Fedor Selivanov/Shutterstock.com; pp. 14–15 Carlos Caetano/Shutterstock.com; p. 16 Adriano Castelli/Shutterstock.com; p. 18 lexan/Shutterstock.com; p. 19 Dariusz Majgier/Shutterstock.com; pp. 21, 22 Bloomberg/Getty Images; p. 26 Jonathan Ferrey/Getty Images; p. 27 Doug Benc/Getty Images; pp. 28–29 Philip Lange/Shutterstock.com.

Library of Congress Cataloging-in-Publication Data

425 5309

Mulligan, Simon, 1977-
  Porsche / by Simon Mulligan. — 1st ed.
    p. cm. — (Speed machines)
  Includes index.
  ISBN 978-1-4488-7456-9 (library binding) — ISBN 978-1-4488-7528-3 (pbk.) —
  ISBN 978-1-4488-7603-7 (6-pack)
  1. Porsche automobiles—History—Juvenile literature. 2. Porsche, Ferdinand, 1875-1951—Juvenile literature. I. Title.
  TL215.P75M85 2013
  629.222—dc23
                                        2011049571

Manufactured in the United States of America

CPSIA Compliance Information: Batch #B4S12PK: For Further Information contact Rosen Publishing, New York, New York at 1-800-237-9932

Contents

What's in a Name?

Most people have a pretty good idea what a Porsche looks like. That is how powerful the Porsche brand is. The name alone creates a picture in your mind. Not all Porsche models look the same, but they all are **designed** in a way that you can tell that each one is a Porsche. Porsche is known for making high-performance, or fast and powerful, cars.

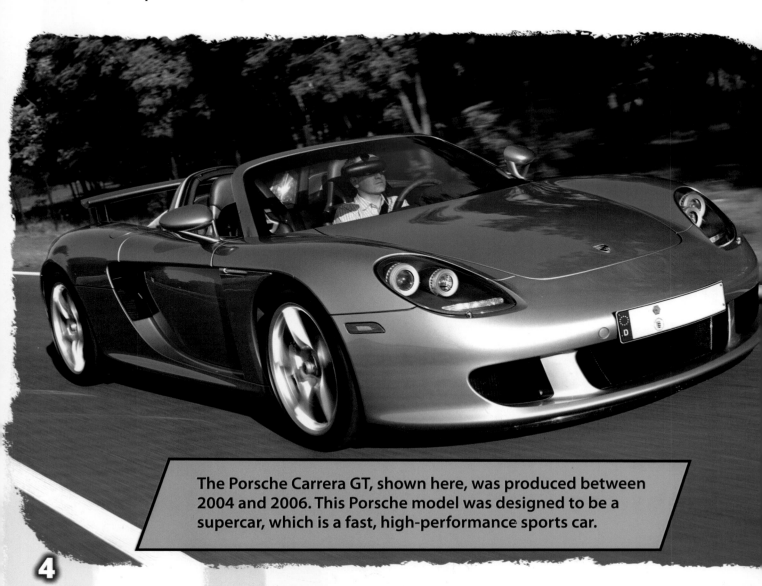

The Porsche Carrera GT, shown here, was produced between 2004 and 2006. This Porsche model was designed to be a supercar, which is a fast, high-performance sports car.

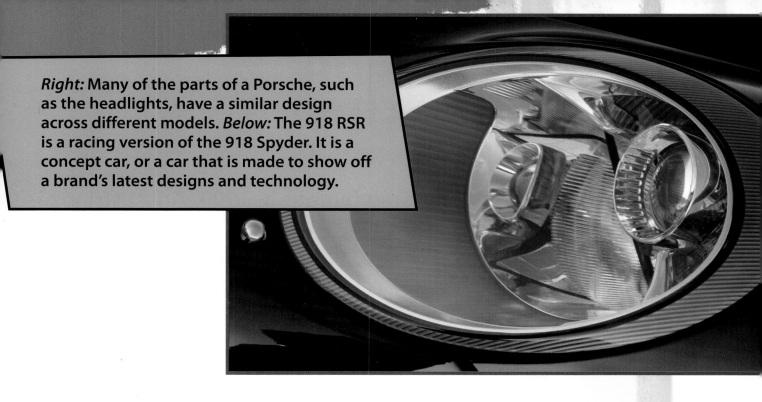

Right: Many of the parts of a Porsche, such as the headlights, have a similar design across different models. *Below:* The 918 RSR is a racing version of the 918 Spyder. It is a concept car, or a car that is made to show off a brand's latest designs and technology.

Porsche might make the most famous sports and **luxury** cars in the world. It also makes some of the most expensive! It is not unusual for a Porsche to cost more than $200,000! One of the reasons these cars cost so much is that they are well made, with a lot of attention paid to every detail.

Porsche makes some of the most beloved cars ever built. The Porsche family has a rich history with cars that goes back over 100 years!

Ferdinand and Ferry Porsche

The name Porsche became famous in 1900. An Austrian **engineer** named Ferdinand Porsche designed a car that was presented at the World's Fair in Paris, France. Porsche's first model ran on electricity. It went only about 35 miles per hour (56 km/h), but at the time that was fast enough to set speed records!

Later, when the gas-powered **internal combustion engine** was invented, Porsche was able to design faster cars. In 1923, Porsche moved to Stuttgart, Germany, where he started a consulting company to develop racecars.

This is the body of the Porsche 64 in the Porsche Museum, in Germany. This car was built around 1938 and is considered the basis from which early Porsches were designed. Only three were ever made!

Here is Porsche founder Ferdinand Porsche around 1940.

The first car built and sold by the Porsche company was the 356, which was introduced in 1948. Porsche had a son also named Ferdinand, who went by the nickname Ferry. The younger Porsche proved to have as much genius for cars as his father. He ran the company after his father's death, in 1951, and remained involved in the company until his death, in 1998.

Built for Speed

Both Ferdinand and Ferry Porsche loved to make racecars. They knew that people would pay lots of money for fast, sleek sports cars. Since Porsche's beginnings, both its racecars and its sports cars have been designed for speed.

For example, the **ignition** for most cars sold in America is on the right, at the base of the steering wheel. On Porsches, the ignition is to the left of the

The 997 Turbo was made between 2006 and 2011.

Porsche is known for making high-performance engines. This is the engine of a 1989 911 Carrera.

steering wheel, on the dashboard, as it is on racecars. This lets a driver turn the car on and shift into gear almost at the same time.

Over the years, the Porsche company has stayed true to its sporty origins. Porsche engineers combine light frames with the most powerful engines they can create. This means a Porsche **accelerates** faster than most other cars on the road.

Designing Sports Cars

In the 1930s, Ferdinand Porsche was involved in the design of the Volkswagen Beetle. When Porsche began designing cars for his own company, he used this design as a starting point. Using Volkswagen parts and the original Volkswagen design, Ferry Porsche created a faster, lighter version of the Beetle. The new sports car was ready in 1948. Ferry called it the 356.

The Panamera is available as a hybrid car. A hybrid car runs on both electricity and gas.

Many sports car lovers prefer convertibles. This is a 2005 911 Carrera GT.

People went crazy for the 356. Not only was it more beautiful than other cars on the road, it was also much more **aerodynamic**. This means it was designed to move with less drag from the air around it. Porsche continued in this direction with other models. The company introduced the Porsche 911 in 1963. Once again, Ferry created the car of the future by improving upon his company's previous designs. Porsche has been doing this ever since.

Racecars

Porsche might be best known for its sports cars, but it is also the biggest **manufacturer** of racecars in the world. Ferdinand Porsche loved racecars. He even raced some of the models himself.

Porsche has stayed true to its roots. Today the company builds some of the fastest cars in the world. This is not just because races are fun. Engineers and scientists at Porsche work hard to break new ground in car design and performance.

This is a 918 RSR, which is Porsche's first hybrid racecar.

The RS Spyder is a Le Mans prototype racecar. This car is often used in endurance races.

Since it was first produced in 1963, the popular Porsche 911 became the basis for Porsche's most successful racecars. The company made many **variations** on the 911 to create faster and faster cars. The 911 GT1, first produced in 1996, is one of the fastest cars Porsche ever created. Since 2005, the Porsche RS Spyder has made a name for itself by winning some of the biggest races in the world.

Racing

The cars Porsche makes for racing are different from the cars it sells to the public. Racecars are driven only by racecar drivers, who are specially trained to be able to drive these high-performing cars at high speeds. Porsche creates different kinds of cars for different kinds of car racing.

The most popular American auto races are NASCAR races. Porsche has designed successful NASCAR models, including the new hybrid Panamera. NASCAR races may last only a couple hours. These are shorter competitions than other styles of car races. The 24 Hours of Le Mans is the oldest **endurance** race in the world. Cars race for 24 hours. They have to be fast, but they also have to run for a long time without breaking down. This is the kind of race that Porsche designers are great at creating cars for.

A 997 GT3 RSR won the 2011 24 Hours Nürburgring, in Germany.

Porsche 356

The 356 was Porsche's first automobile built for production. This means that the company created models to sell. The 356 was first sold in 1948, but it did not become popular for several years. By the 1950s, it was one of the best-regarded cars on the market. People were delighted at how easily the 356 handled. It was also faster and better built than most other sports cars on the market.

This is a 1956 Porsche 356, which was designed by Ferry Porsche.

Porsche 356

Engine size	3.4 liters
Number of cylinders	6
Transmission	Manual
Gearbox	6 speeds
0–60 mph (0–97 km/h)	4.8 seconds
Top speed	171 mph (275 km/h)

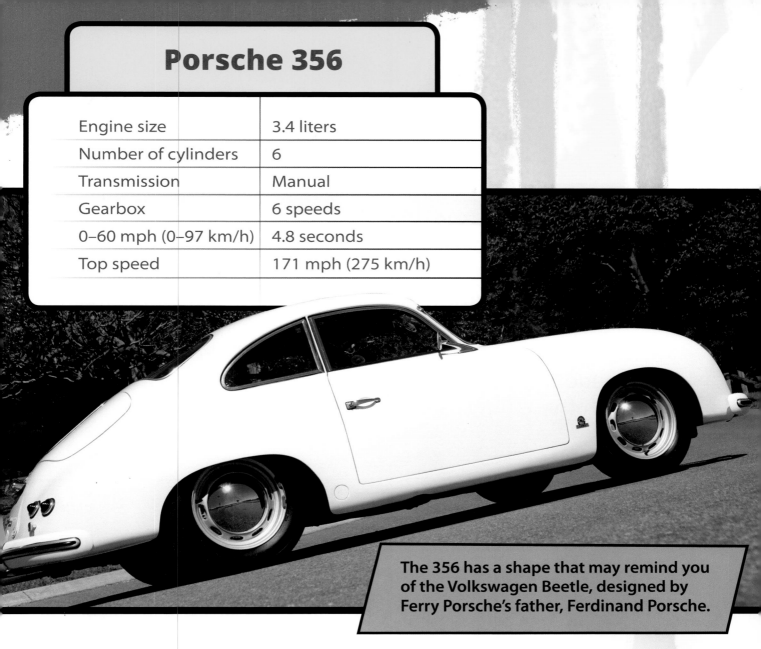

The 356 has a shape that may remind you of the Volkswagen Beetle, designed by Ferry Porsche's father, Ferdinand Porsche.

Although the first 356 model began with Volkswagen parts, Porsche quickly improved upon the car and made it fully its own. The 356 featured a four-**cylinder** rear engine. This simply means that the engine was in the back of the car. It also had **rear-wheel drive**. Like most sports cars, the 356 had two doors. Later models featured **convertible** roofs. The fastest 356 model was the Speedster. It could reach 112 miles per hour (180 km/h).

Porsche 911

In the 1950s and 1960s, sports cars became very popular all over the world. Other car companies began to make cars that were bigger, faster, and better performing than the 356. They were bigger, and they could go faster. Some of them did not cost nearly as much as the 356. Porsche needed to design a new sports car to compete with these new cars.

The 911 is the Porsche model with the longest production history. Shown here is a 2010 GT2 RS model.

2012 911 Turbo S

Engine size	3.8 liters
Number of cylinders	6
Transmission	Dual clutch
Gearbox	7 speeds
0–60 mph (0–97 km/h)	3.1 seconds
Top speed	196 mph (315 km/h)

Here is a 1973 911 Targa.

That next great Porsche model was the 911, and it went on sale in 1963. Most sports cars of the day had four speeds. The 911 had five. It was also fast! The new engine allowed it to go from 0 to 60 miles per hour (0–97 km/h) in just 9 seconds! The 911 did more than just replace the 356. It also outsold the original car. Today, the 911 remains Porsche's best-selling model and is faster than earlier generations of the car.

Boxster

Porsche is constantly designing and testing new car models. It is also proud of its history and likes to design its new cars to keep some of the same features as older models. One of the Boxster's inspirations was the Porsche 550 Spyder, which was made from 1953 until 1956. The Boxster is known as a roadster. A roadster is a car with two seats and a convertible roof. Its engine is called a "boxer" because of its shape. If you combine the words "boxer" and "roadster," you get "Boxster."

Here is a Boxster with its top down.

Today, the fastest Boxsters can top speeds of 170 miles per hour (274 km/h)!

2012 Boxster S

Engine size	3.4 liters
Number of cylinders	6
Transmission	Manual
Gearbox	6 speeds
0–60 mph (0–97 km/h)	4.8 seconds
Top speed	171 mph (275 km/h)

The first Boxster hit the roads in 1996. It had a powerful 2.5-liter, six-cylinder engine. As always, Porsche worked to improve the new models. In 2000, the Boxster had a bigger engine, could go faster, and could handle better. The outward appearance of the Boxster looks very much like the 550 Spyder racecar. Car buyers love the Boxster because of its classic look.

Cayman

Car buyers loved the look of the Boxster, but roadsters are not practical cars for everyone. They have limited trunk space. Convertible roofs are not useful for drivers who live in cold and rainy parts of the world. Porsche launched the Cayman in 2006 as the perfect car for people who love the look of the Boxster but do not want to own a roadster.

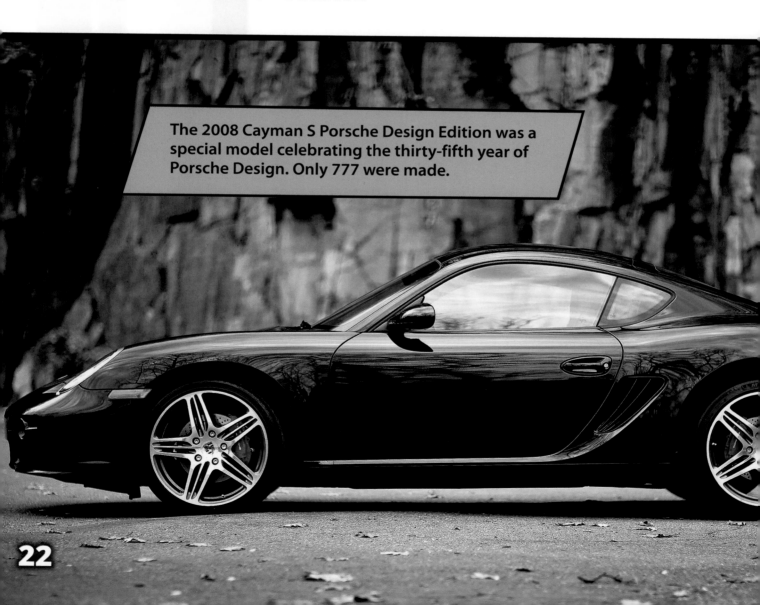

The 2008 Cayman S Porsche Design Edition was a special model celebrating the thirty-fifth year of Porsche Design. Only 777 were made.

2012 Cayman R

Engine size	3.4 liters
Number of cylinders	6
Transmission	Manual
Gearbox	6 speeds
0–60 mph (0–97 km/h)	4.7 seconds
Top speed	175 mph (282 km/h)

The Cayman is a coupe, or a closed-body car. The first Cayman models looked very much like the Boxster. In fact, they even had the same fenders, headlights, and interior. The first Caymans were built with the same **suspension**, too. One key difference is the Cayman's large hatchback, which allows drivers to carry bags, suitcases, and other items. The Cayman proved to be another hit for Porsche's engineers. It won several major awards.

Cayenne

Most sports cars have only two seats. What if you want to carry more passengers? Porsche decided it was time to make a **sport-utility vehicle**, or SUV. The Cayenne is not as big as some SUVs, but it does have room to seat up to five people. Other Porsches had six-cylinder engines, but this bigger car needed a bigger engine. The Cayenne became the first Porsche to feature an eight-cylinder, or V8, engine.

The first Porsche Cayenne model went on sale in 2002. Newer models have become smaller and faster. The 2011 Cayenne offers a **hybrid** model, which runs on both gas

The Cayenne is sometimes called a crossover vehicle. A crossover has the taller, roomier body of an SUV but is built on a car platform.

2012 Cayenne Turbo

Engine size	4.8 liters
Number of cylinders	8
Transmission	Manual
Gearbox	8 speeds
0–60 mph (0–97 km/h)	4.4 seconds
Top speed	172 mph (277 km/h)

The Cayenne was the best-selling Porsche model in 2012.

and electricity. This means it burns less gas than other SUVs. This saves money at the gas pump, and it is also good for the planet. The Cayenne is built for families rather than for speed. It is still pretty fast for an SUV!

RS Spyder

Porsche enjoyed years of racing success with the Porsche 911 GT1. It retired that model from racing in 1999 to develop something even faster. Named after Porsche's 550 Spyder of the 1950s, the new RS Spyder raced and won first place in its class for the first time at the American Le Mans Series in 2005.

Here are two RS Spyders at the 2007 Monterey Sports Car Championships, in California.

RS Spyder

Engine size	3.4 liters
Number of cylinders	8
Transmission	Semiautomatic
Gearbox	6 speeds
Weight	1,820 pounds (825 kg)

The "RS" in this car's name stands for "renn sport." This is German for "race sport."

In 2008, the Spyder won the 12 Hours of Sebring Race. Porsche was back on top of the endurance racing world. Engineers worked hard to make the Spyder so fast. Instead of using older Porsche models, they built a brand new V8 engine from scratch. The RS Spyder can go from 0 to 60 miles per hour (0–97 km/h) in about 3 seconds, and it can attain speeds of almost 200 miles per hour (322 km/h).

Other Porsche Models

Throughout its history, Porsche has improved its cars by making newer models lighter, faster, and sportier. Car fans cannot wait to see what Porsche engineers are working on next. In fact, some people break the law to take photos secretly of new Porsche cars being built and tested!

The 911 continues to be Porsche's most loved car. Porsche even tried to stop making the model so it could focus on other things. Car buyers were so unhappy that Porsche decided to keep making new 911s.

The next 911s, Cayennes, Boxsters, and Caymans will be made of a special light metal called aluminum, which will make the cars lighter still. It will also help them get even better gas **mileage**. No one knows what Porsche will do next, but car buyers know its new models will be fast, well built, and beautiful.

Porsche showed off its latest designs at the Essen Motor Show, in Germany, in 2011.

Comparing Porsches

CAR	YEARS MADE	2010 SALES*	TOP SPEED	FUN FACT
356	1948–1965	n/a **	112 mph (180 km/h)	The first 356 rolled out of the factory on June 8, 1948.
911	1963–	6,839	196 mph (315 km/h)	The 911's original name was the 901, but Peugeot already had the rights to that name.
Boxster	1996–	1,909	171 mph (275 km/h)	The Boxster has its cylinders laid out flat, rather than in a V shape, as in other cars.
Cayman	2006–	1,986	175 mph (282 km/h)	"Cayman" is another spelling of "caiman." A caiman is a reptile related to alligators and crocodiles.
Cayenne	2002–	7,735	172 mph (277 km/h)	The Cayenne is made using some of the same parts as Volkswagen's Touareg.

* North American sales figures
** Approximately 76,000 356s were sold between 1948 and 1965.

Glossary

accelerates (ik-SEH-luh-rayts) Increases in speed.

aerodynamic (er-oh-dy-NA-mik) Made to move through the air easily.

convertible (kun-VER-tuh-bel) Having a top that can be lowered or taken off.

cylinder (SIH-len-der) The enclosed space for a piston in an engine.

designed (dih-ZYND) Planned the form of something.

endurance (en-DUR-ints) The ability to go long distances without breaking down.

engineer (en-juh-NEER) A master at planning and building engines, machines, roads, and bridges.

hybrid (HY-brud) Cars that have an engine that runs on gasoline and a motor that runs on electricity.

ignition (ig-NIH-shun) The tool that causes the spark that makes a car engine start.

internal combustion engine (in-TUR-nel kum-BUS-chun EN-jin) An engine that runs by burning a fuel.

luxury (LUK-shuh-ree) Comforts and beauties of life that are not necessary.

manufacturer (man-yuh-FAK-cher-er) People who make something by hand or with a machine.

mileage (MY-lij) The number of miles a car can travel on a gallon of gas.

rear-wheel drive (REER-hweel DRYV) When the engine is in the front of a car and the wheels that are controlled by the driver are in the back.

sport-utility vehicle (sport-yoo-TIH-luh-tee VEE-uh-kul) A large car that has some characteristics of trucks.

suspension (suh-SPENT-shun) A shock-absorbing system in a car or motorcycle.

variations (ver-ee-AY-shunz) Different ways of doing things.

Index

Websites

Due to the changing nature of Internet links, PowerKids Press has developed an online list of websites related to the subject of this book. This site is updated regularly. Please use this link to access the list: www.powerkidslinks.com/smach/por/